I Remember Love

written by Kathy Wafer

illustrated by Janet Maines

No part of this publication may be reproduced in whole or in part, or stored in a retrieval system, or transmitted in any form or by any means, electronic, mechanical, photocopying, recording, or otherwise, without written permission of the publisher. For information regarding permission, write to DiggyPOD, 301 Industrial Drive, Tecumseh, MI 49286.

ISBN 979-8-218-22253-6

Text copyright © 2023 by Kathy Wafer
Cover, Internal Illustrations, and Design copyright ©2023 by Janet Maines
All rights reserved.
Published by DiggyPOD
301 Industrial Drive, Tecumseh, MI 49286
877-944-7844 (Toll Free)
734-429-3309 (Fax)
DiggyPOD.com

Printed in the United States of America

To my husband, Corry,
daughters, Jessica and Madeline,
sons-in-law, Cody and Daniel
and grandchildren –
Daniel, Cora, Lucy, Betty and Jude.

I remember the LOVE
I felt finding out about you.

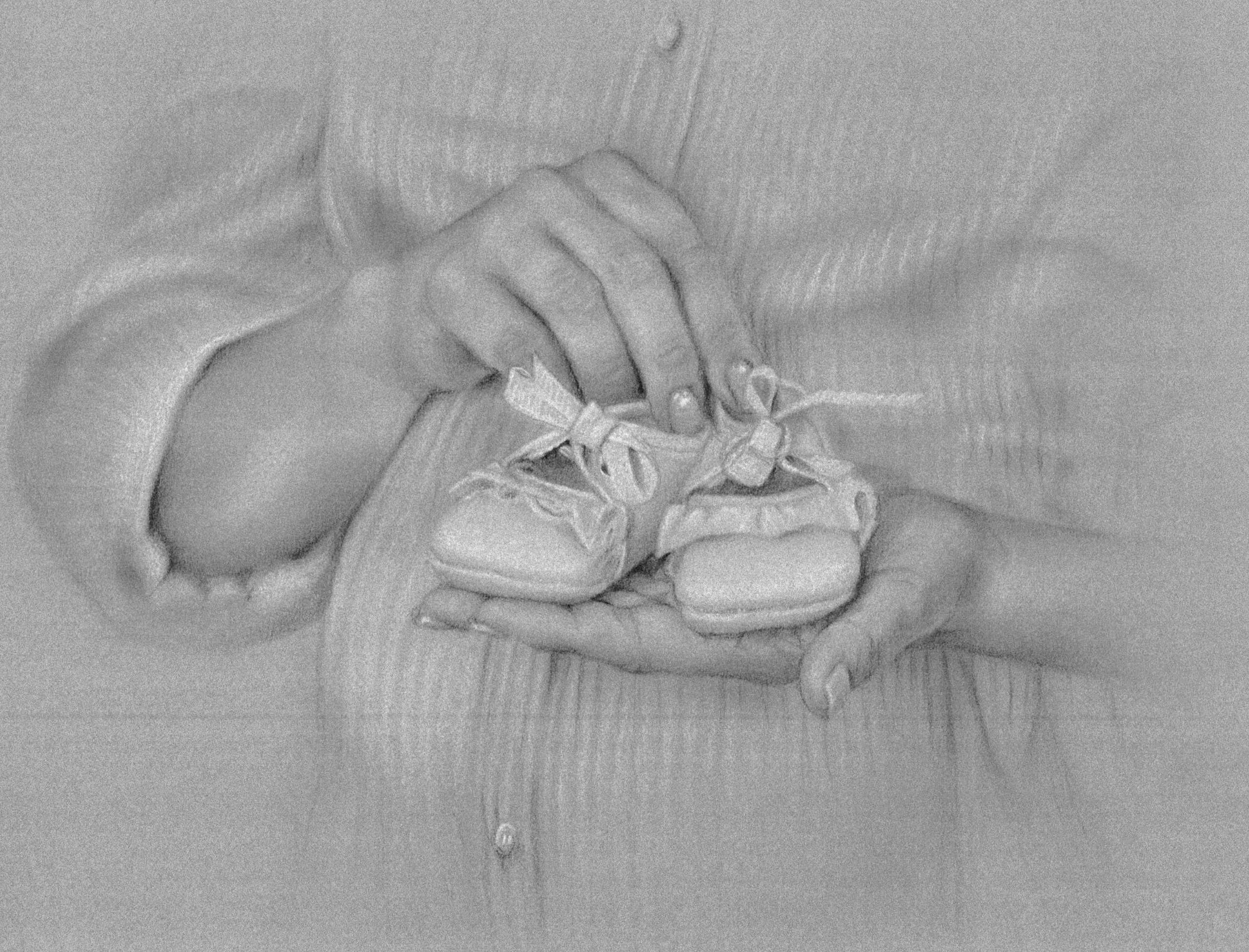

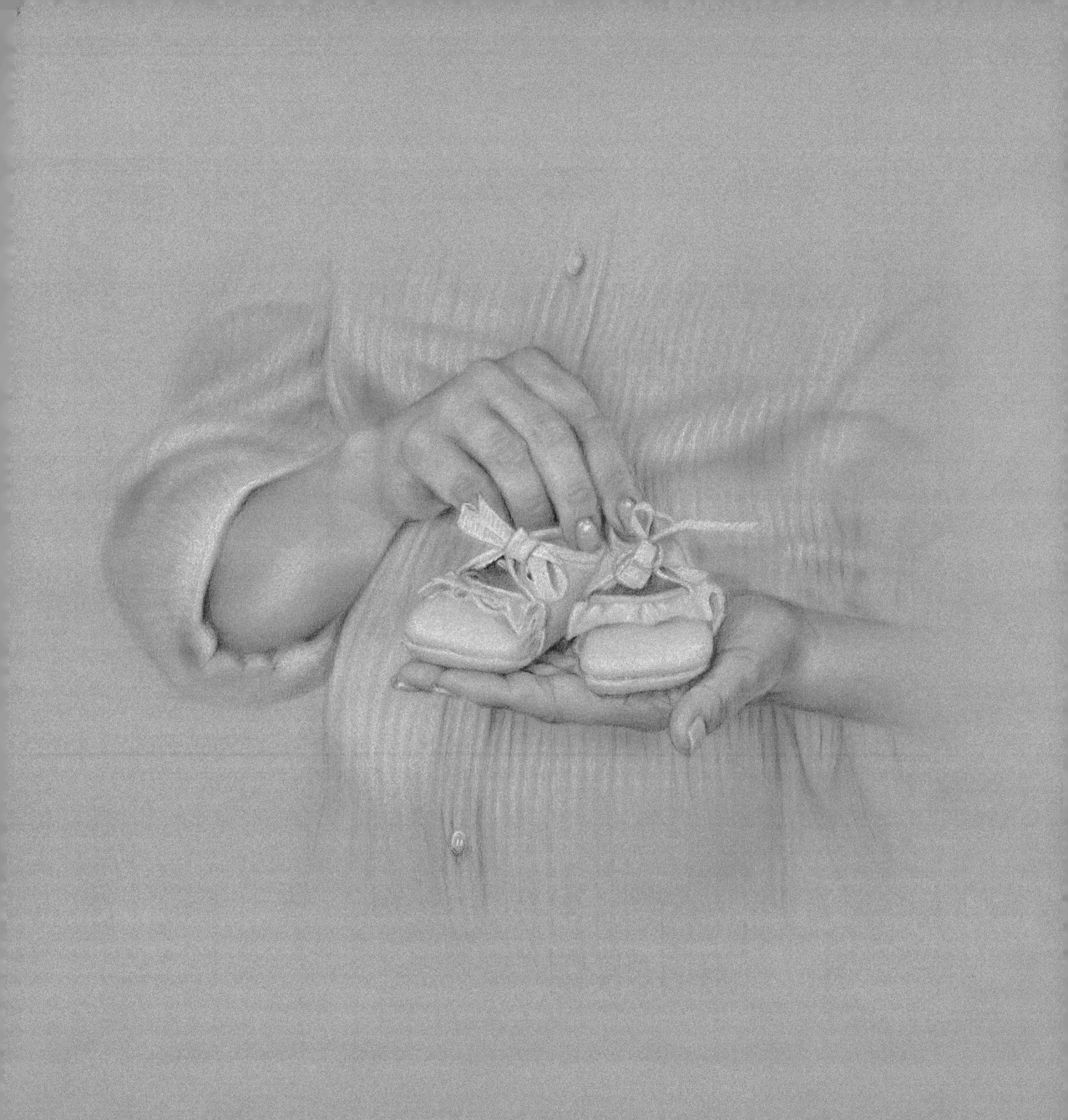

I remember the LOVE
of seeing you for the first time.

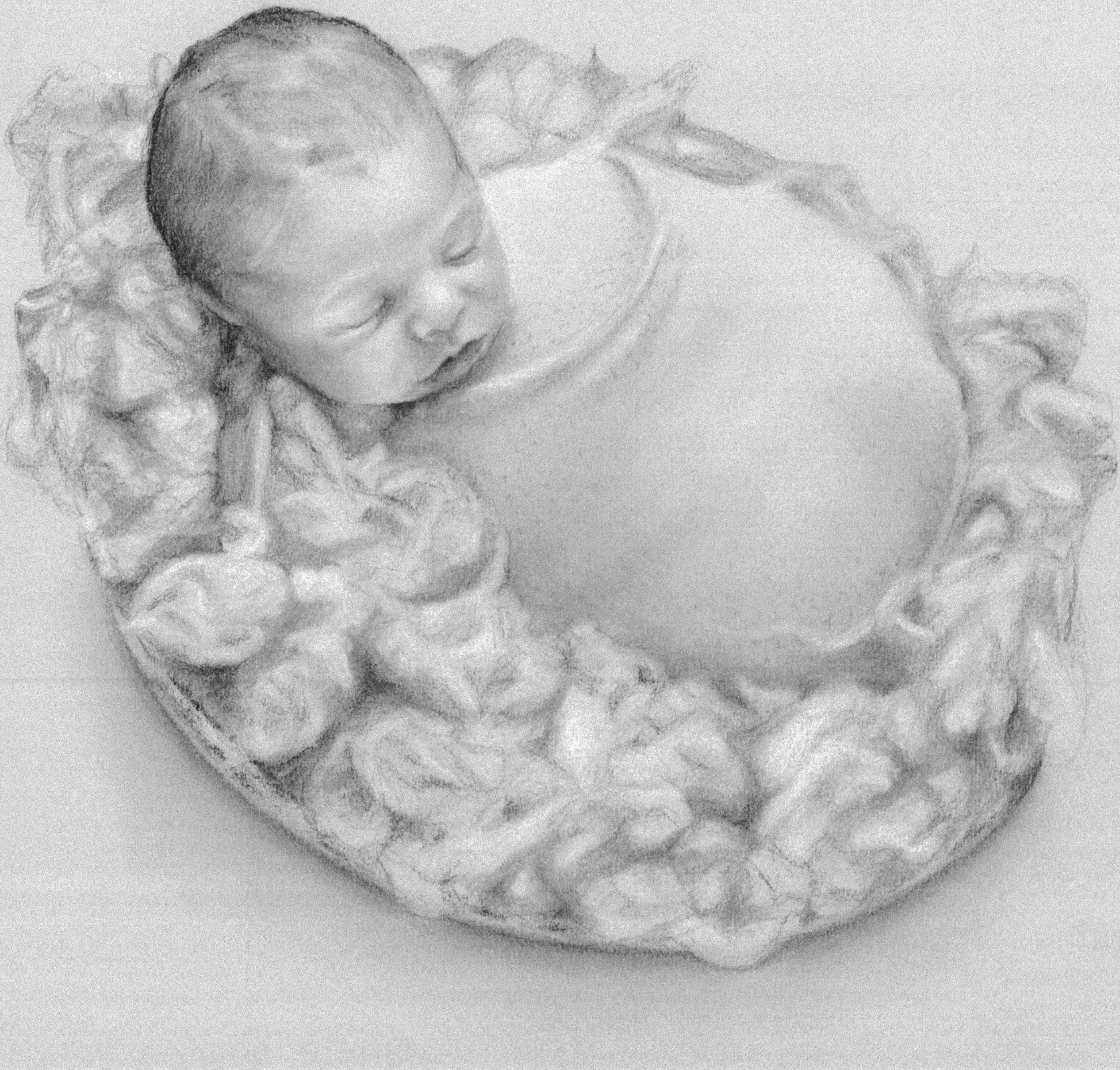

I remember the LOVE
of watching you take your first steps.

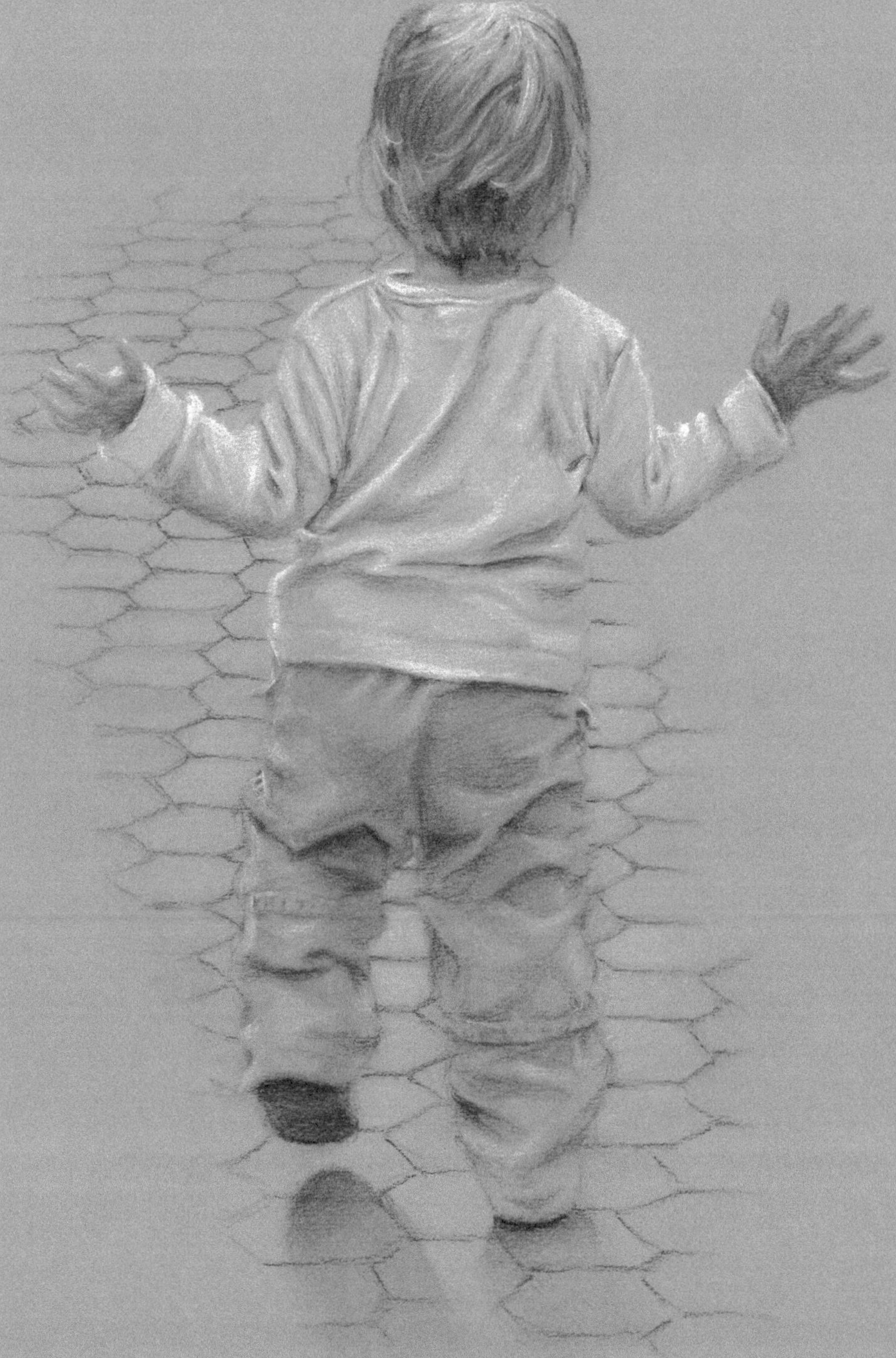

I remember the LOVE
of seeing your fingerprints left on my table.

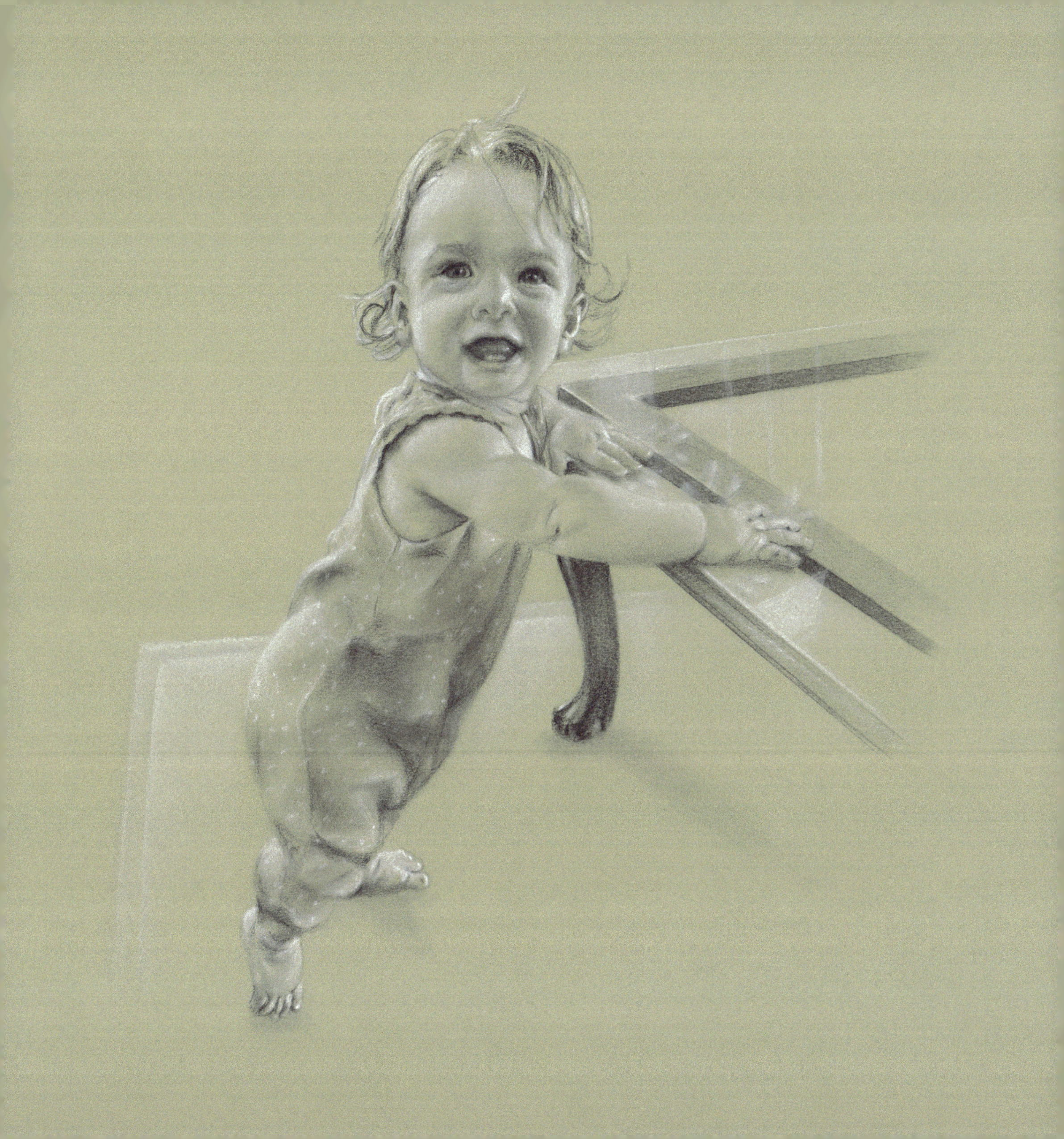

I remember the LOVE
of watching you play in fall leaves.

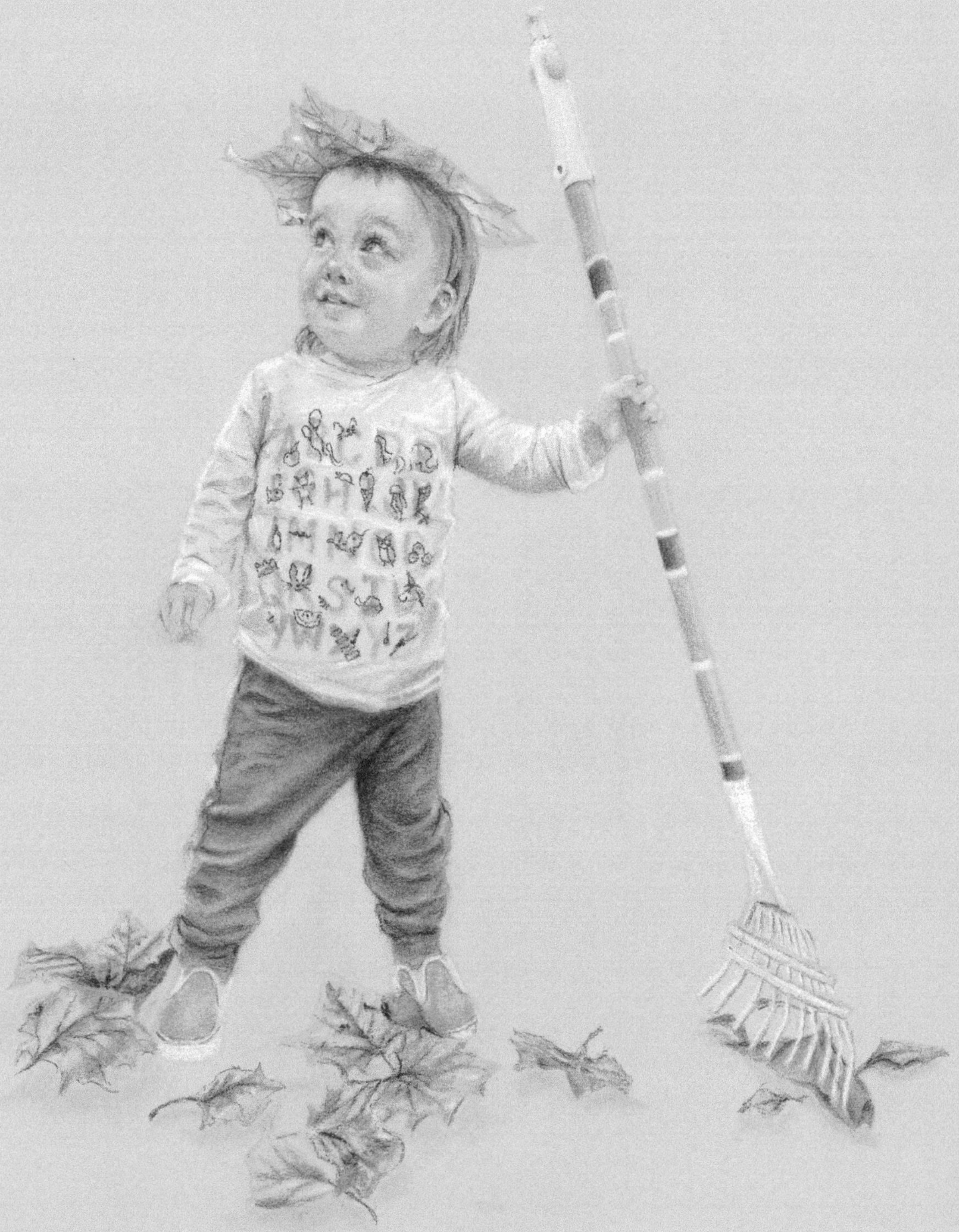

I remember the LOVE
of making snow angels with you.

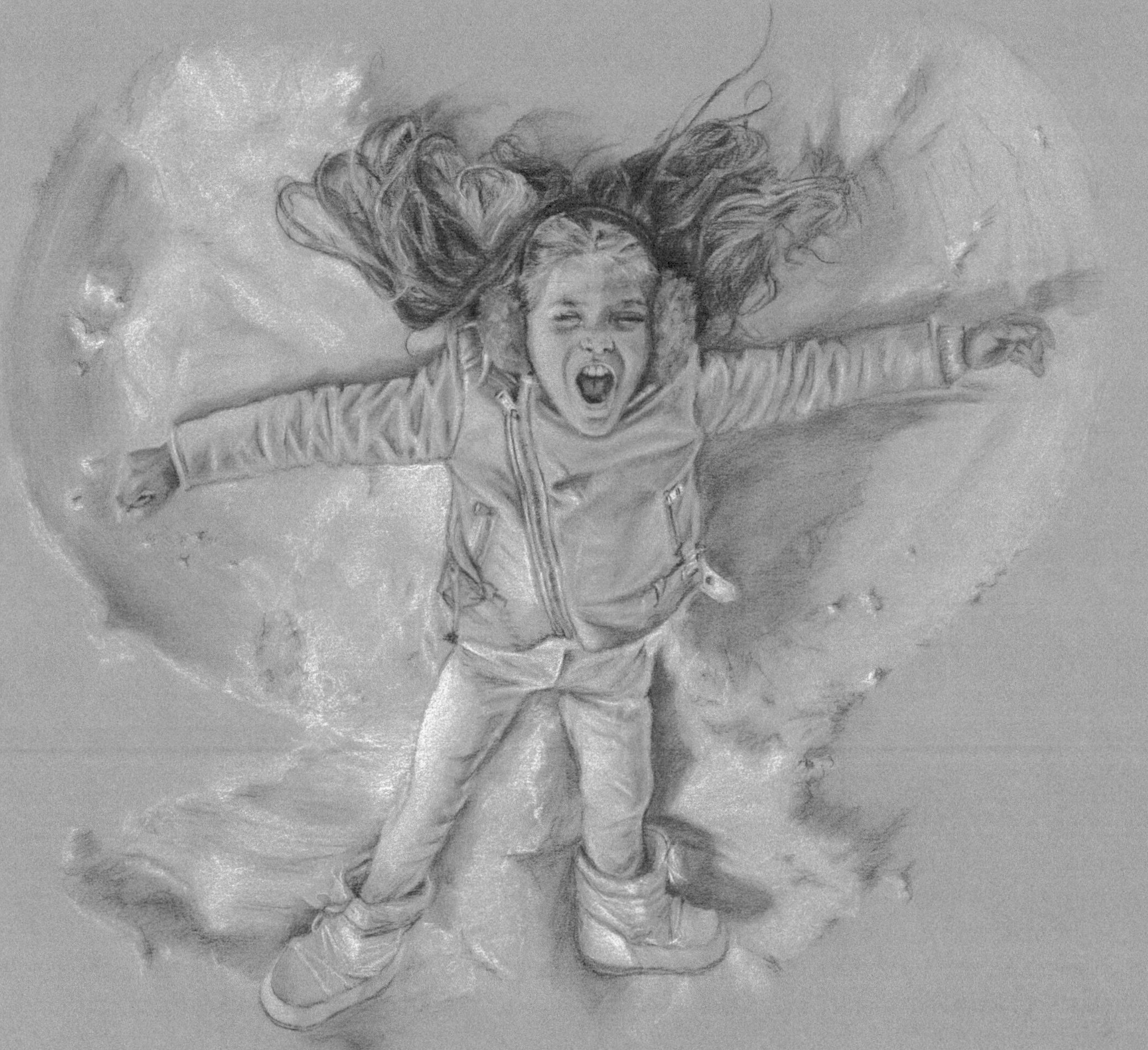

I remember the LOVE
of you reading to me.

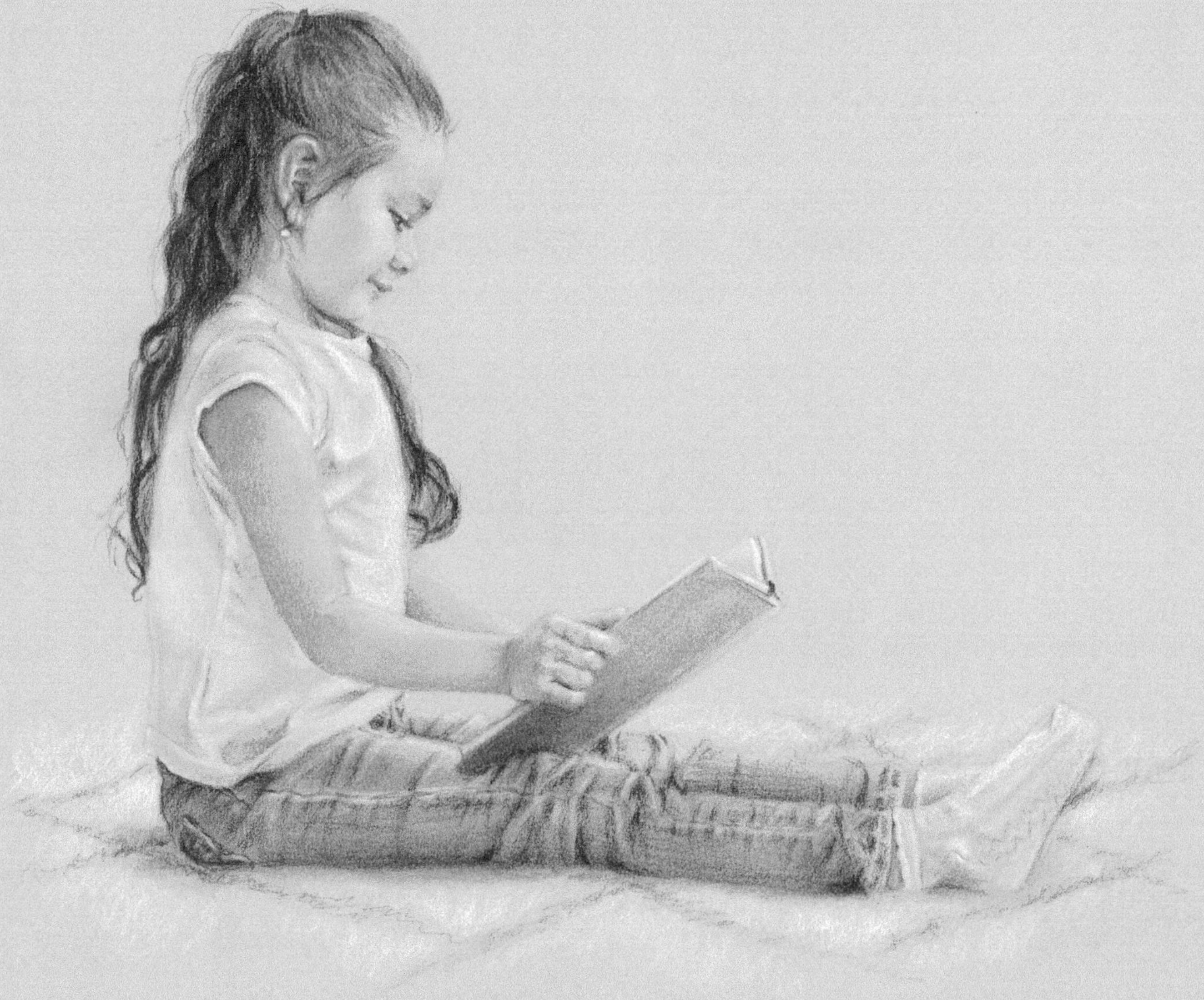

I remember the LOVE
of cheering as your number one fan.

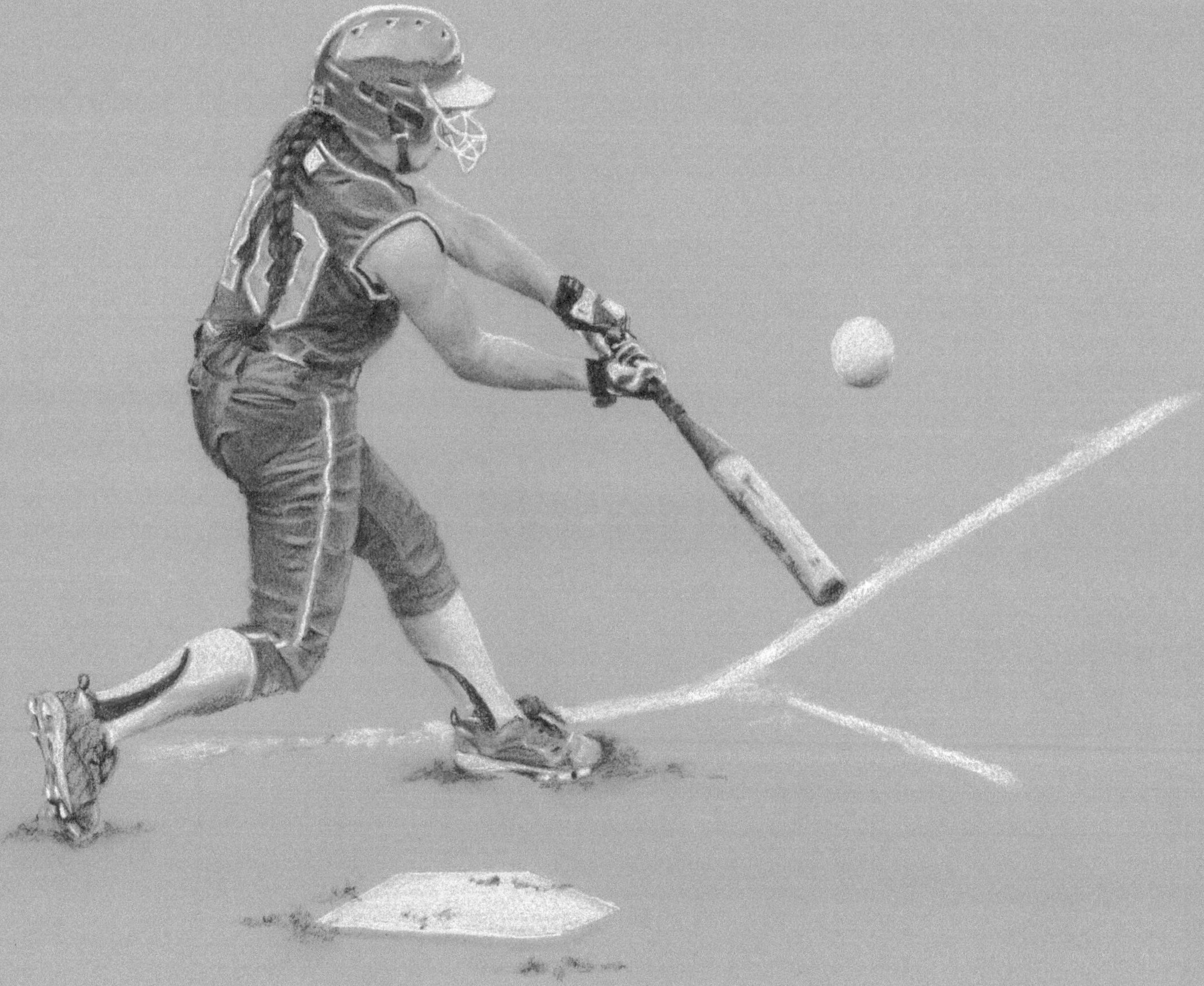

I remember the LOVE
of seeing you excited about Senior Prom.

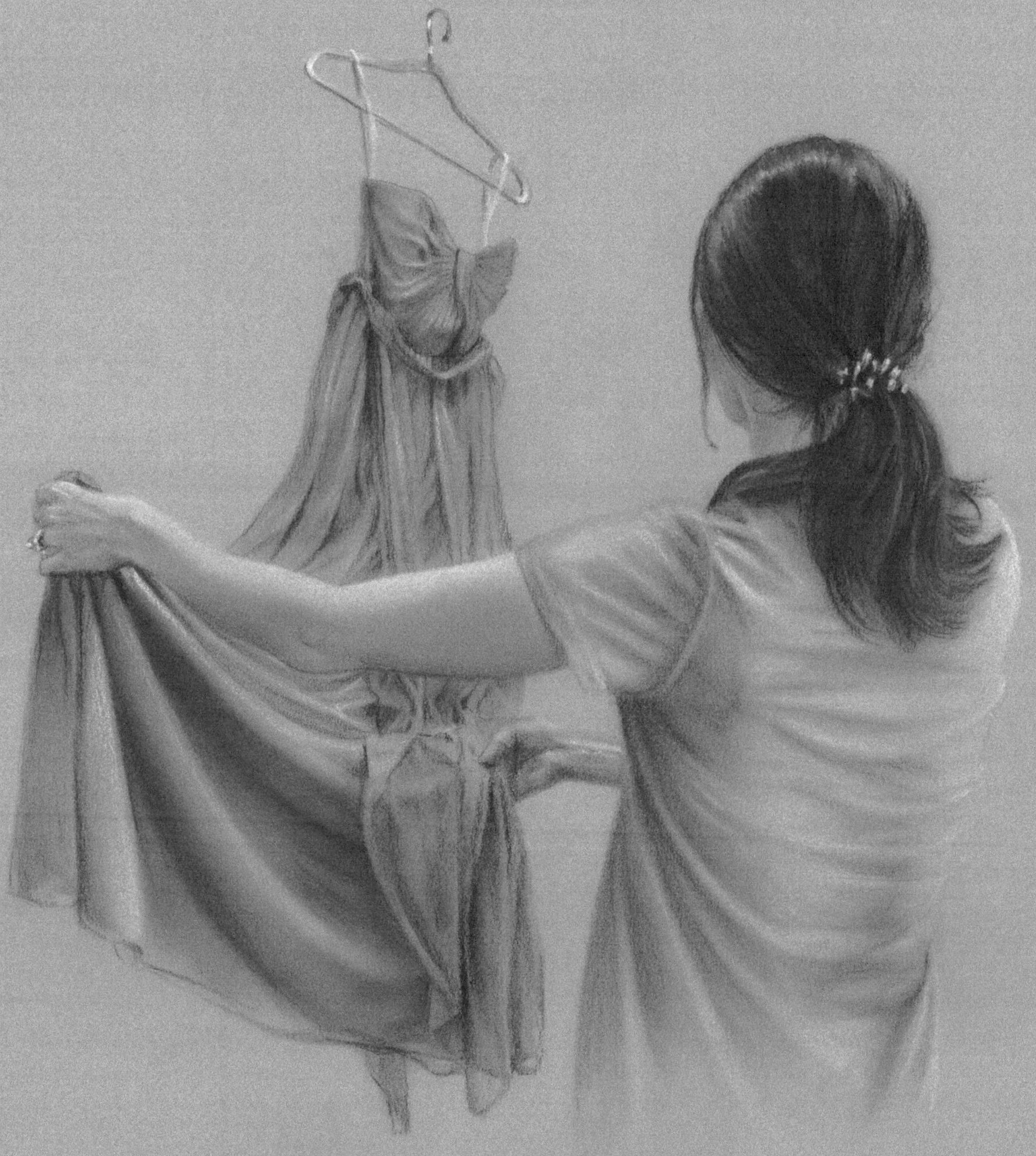

I remember the LOVE
of us dancing, even when no music was playing.

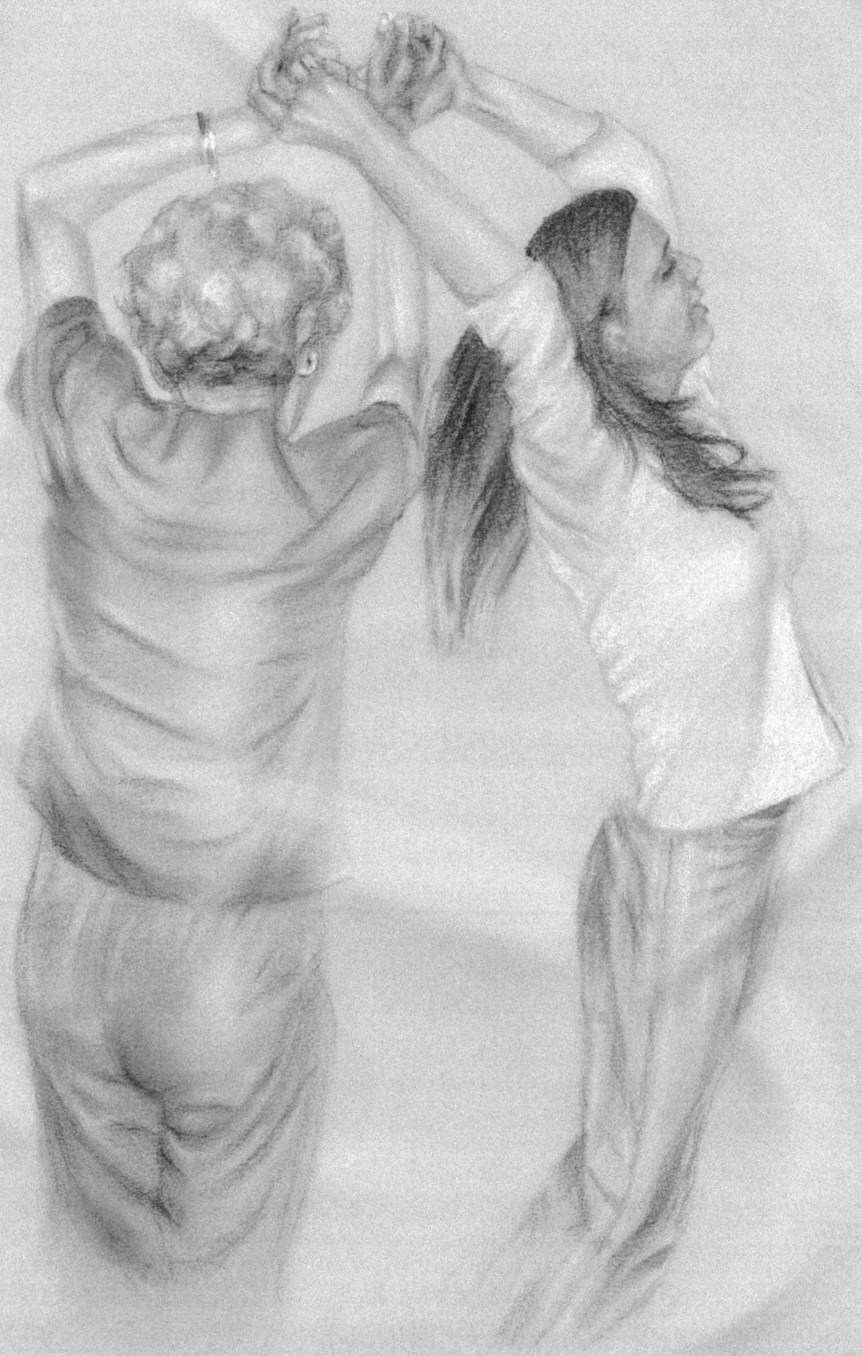

I remember the LOVE
of attending your college graduation.

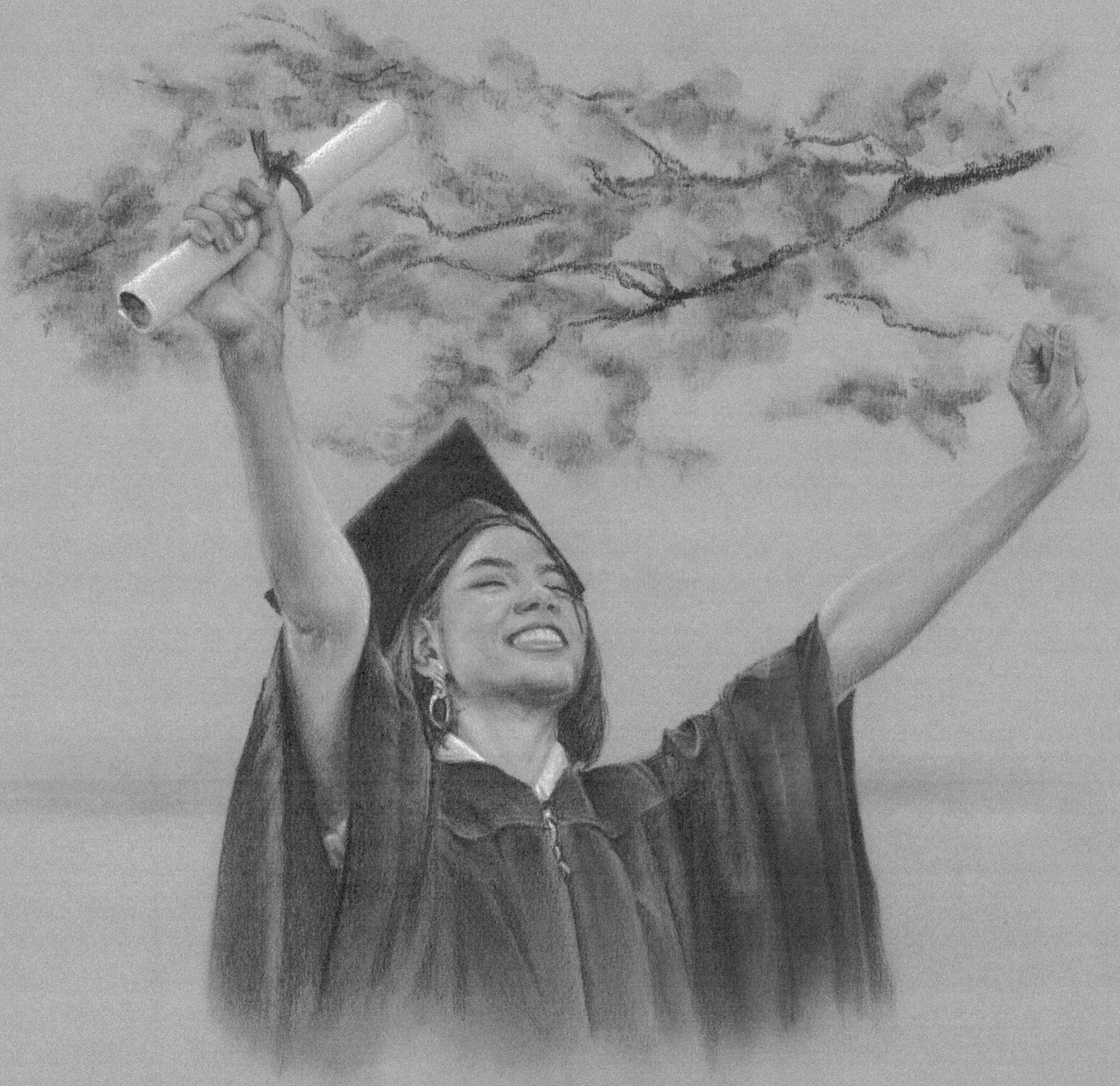

I remember the LOVE
of crying happy tears on your wedding day.

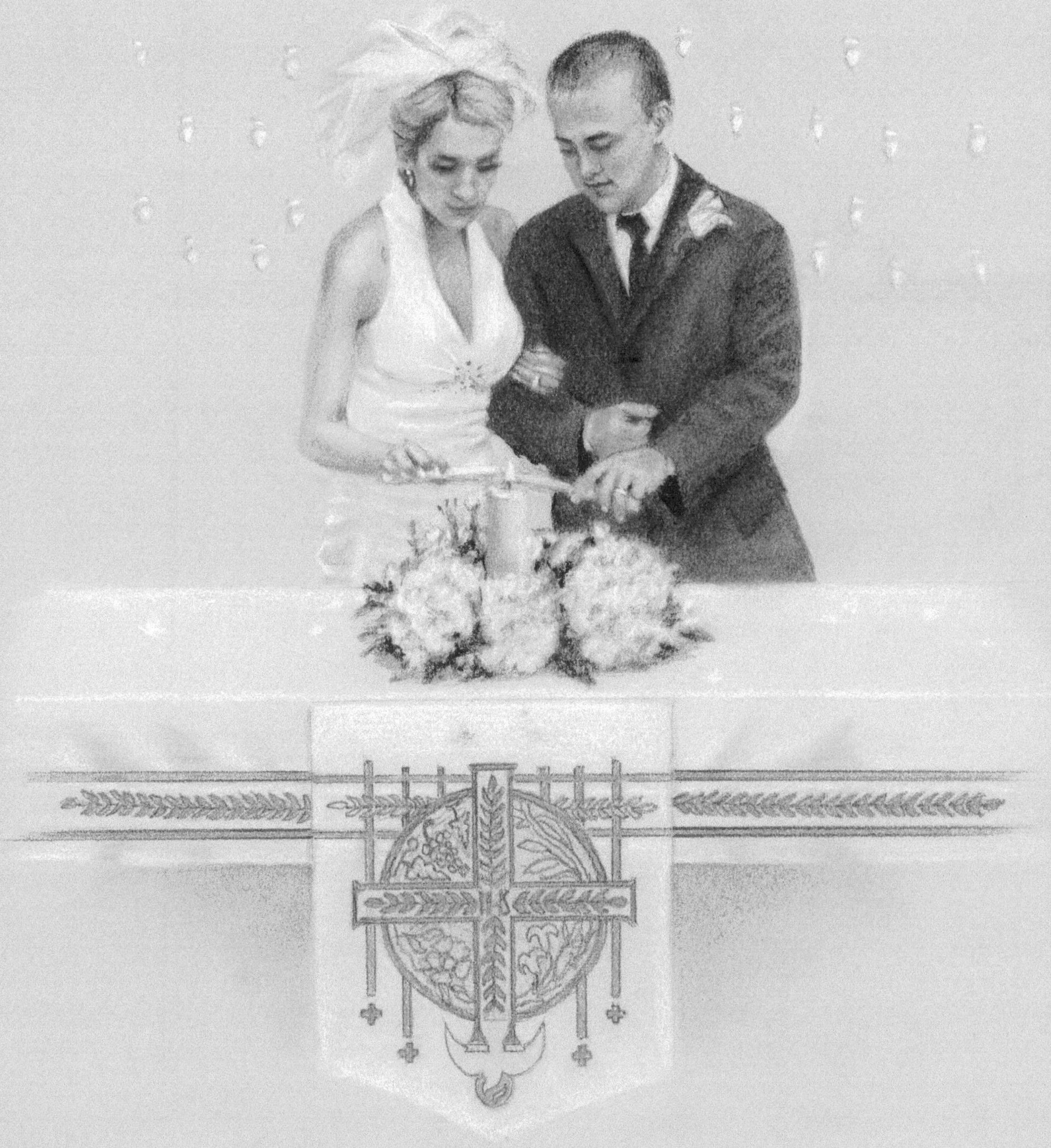

I remember the LOVE
of sharing family stories from these photos.

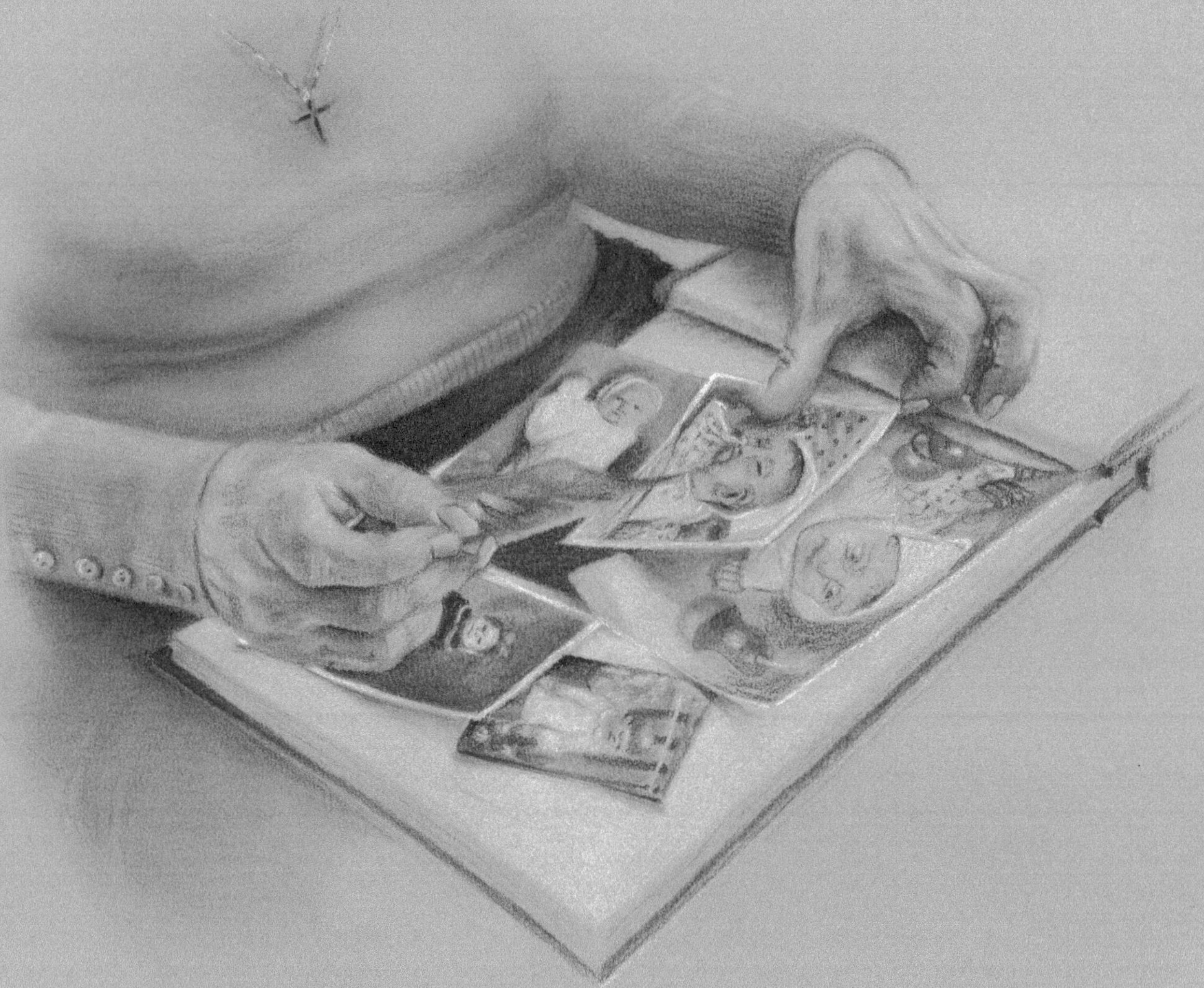

I remember the LOVE,

but honey, I can't remember your name.

Even though my memory fades,
still...

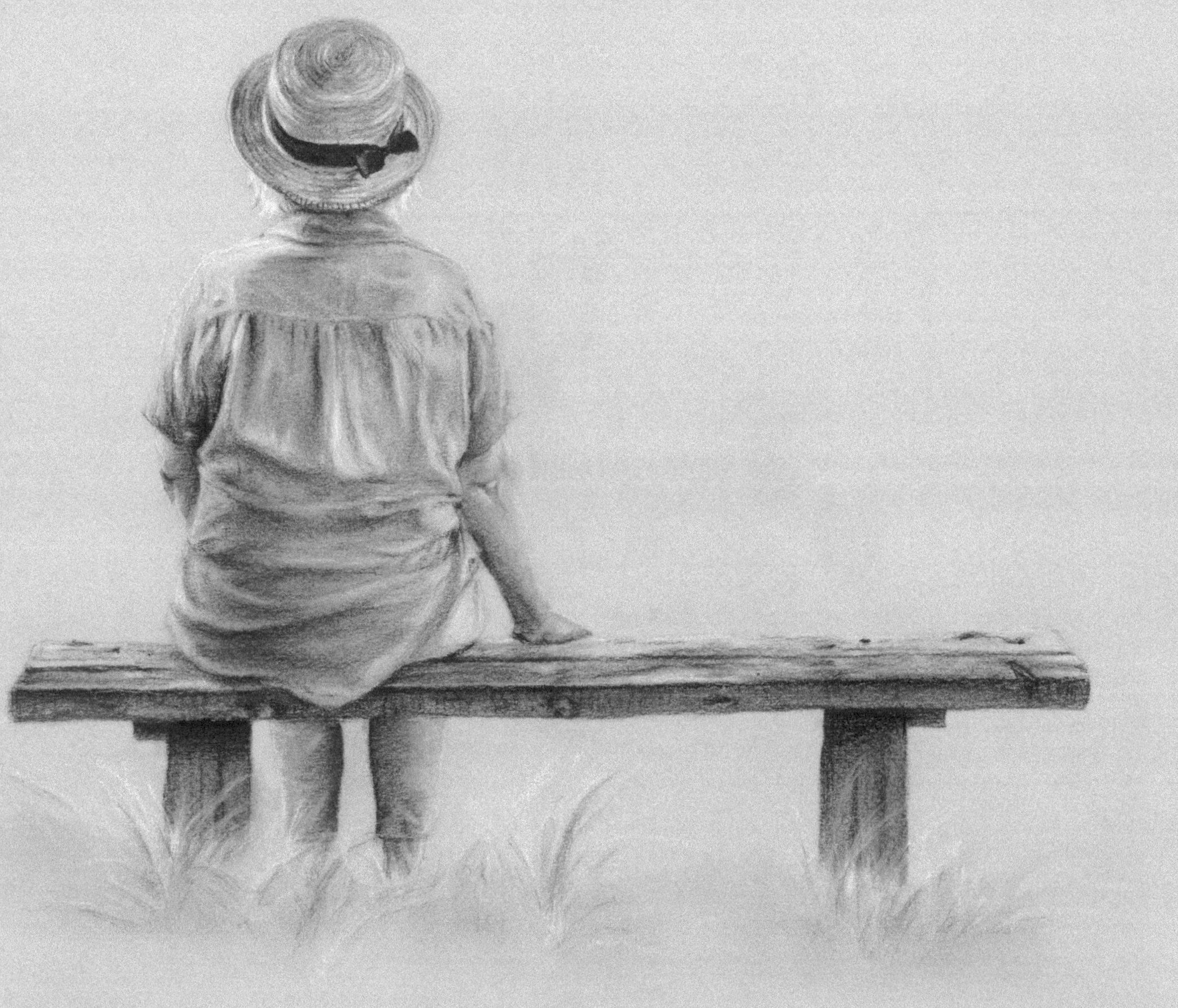

I remember...LOVE.

Love always protects, always trusts,
always hopes, always perseveres.
Love never fails.

- 1 Corinthians 13:7-8

In loving memory of my mother,
Catherine Hollingsworth Snare.